Pa...
for Adults

LEARNING
TO STUDY THE
BIBLE

L. J. Zimmerman

ABINGDON PRESS

Nashville

Editorial/Design Team

Erin Floyd	Editor
Madeline Walls	Production Editor
Kent Sneed	Designer

Administrative Team

Rev. Brian K. Milford	President and Publisher
Marjorie M. Pon	Associate Publisher and Editor of Church School Publications (CSP)
Mary M. Mitchell	Design Manager
Brittany Sky	Senior Editor, Children's Resources

Written by: L. J. Zimmerman

Cover Design: Kellie Green; Art: Shutterstock®

LEARNING TO STUDY THE BIBLE: ADULT PARTICIPANT BOOK. An official resource for The United Methodist Church approved by Discipleship Ministries and published by Abingdon Press, a division of The United Methodist Publishing House, 2222 Rosa L. Parks Blvd., Nashville, TN 37288-1306. Price: $8.99. Copyright © 2018 Abingdon Press. All rights reserved. Printed in the United States of America.

18 19 20 21 22 23 24 25 26 27—10 9 8 7 6 5 4 3 2 1

ISBN:9781501871061

PACP10541719-01

 Abingdon Press™

Contents

Introduction

Learning to Study the Bible offers tools needed to explore the Bible using the classic questions: Who? What? When? Where? Why? How?

This curriculum is written with several assumptions about the Bible:

- The Bible is a living text. While it was written hundreds of thousands of years ago, it continues to speak to people of faith today, and is interpreted in a variety of contexts and cultures.
- The Bible was created in a historical context very different from our own. Learning about the historical context of the Bible and its authors enriches our understanding of the text.
- Biblical interpretation is an act of faith, guided by the Holy Spirit.
- Every reader has interpretive lenses, ways of seeing the world that affect his or her interpretation of the text.

- There are many interpretive layers between ourselves and the biblical text, in the form of translators, scribes, copyists, editors, authors, and oral storytellers.

Take a moment to consider what you think about these assumptions. Which of them strike you? What assumptions about the Bible do you bring to this study?

The Bible is an important book in Western culture. References to the Bible abound in books, movies, and popular culture. There are many different teachings, both explicit and implicit, about the Bible and why it matters to our lives. Some teachings have been damaging to people of faith.

What were you taught about the Bible growing up? Did you find your education about the Bible helpful? Why or why not?

Differing interpretations of the Bible have fueled many bitter fights among Christians over the centuries. Even the formation of the biblical canon (the list of books accepted as Holy Scripture) caused a stir!

What are some controversial topics that come up for you when you think about studying the Bible? How can you respond in a loving, encouraging way?

This study helps expand our understandings of how to use the Bible and many of its helpful resources so we can create space to better understand our relationship to Scripture and one another.

1. Who? Author and Audience

Why Does This Matter?

For some Bibles sold online, the author is listed as God. This reference to the divine inspiration of the sacred Scriptures is amusing, but it clouds an important reality. God's word comes to us through real people. The people who created the Scriptures, as we know them, were humans like us: people who told the stories of their faith, wrote them down, edited them, compiled them, and painstakingly copied them over the centuries. The people who created the Bible were deeply invested in their own faith, and in passing on their traditions to others.

What we find in the Bible is the embodied Word of God—embodied by those who originally spoke and wrote the words. God's truth comes to us in human-shaped containers. The humans bearing God's word spoke certain languages, had particular beliefs about the world, and had relationships with their original audiences. Much of that information is lost to us. But what we can discover about the authors of the Scriptures enriches our understanding of the words.

Sometimes the Bible itself tells us about its authors. Psalm 51 is attributed to King David, for example. This psalm of contrition is much more meaningful because we can read up on the backstory (2 Samuel 11–12). Paul's letter to the Philippians is made richer by knowing the story of Paul founding the Philippian church with Lydia (Acts 16:11-40).

In other instances, our ability to get to know the author is guesswork based on the text itself. The Book of Isaiah, for example, is suspected to be composed by three different individuals, then compiled into one prophetic book. Biblical scholars identify these three "Isaiahs" by their writing style, the historical references they include, and the themes they take up. Knowing that the original Isaiah wrote from a crumbling Israelite kingdom, while a later "ghostwriter" wrote from the Babylonian exile, gives the text new shades of meaning.

Knowledge of the people who wrote and received the Bible is one part of interpretation. However, God's word continues to speak in new contexts today. By connecting, even in a small way, with the humans on the other side of the stories, Scripture comes to life in a new way.

WHO WROTE THE BIBLE

Let's start with the basics. The Bible isn't just one book. It's actually a collection of books—like a library. The Bible includes sixty-six books. Does that mean there were sixty-six authors of the Bible? Not exactly.

Some books are collections of stories that used to be passed down orally. Before they were written down, people told the stories around fires, at meals, and before bed. The stories were well-known, and everyone told them in a slightly different way. It would be nearly impossible to identify the true author of these stories. Instead, we call the person who wrote all the stories down the editor.

Another thing that makes it hard to tell exactly how many people wrote the Bible is the use of pseudonyms. Pseudonyms are false names. People might use the name of a more famous person to give their writing more credibility. One example is in the Book of Ecclesiastes. The author claims to be a king of Israel, implying King Solomon, who was known for his wisdom. But evidence suggests that the book was probably written hundreds of years after King Solomon lived.

Pseudonyms weren't always meant to deceive people. Sometimes a prophet gathered followers who learned from the prophet and began to think and speak like the prophet. After the prophet's death, his followers might continue writing under his name. This wasn't considered lying or false. They were simply carrying on the prophet's train of thought. Parts of the Book of Isaiah are thought to be written by one of Isaiah's followers, years after Isaiah first preached.

There is sometimes little we can know about the people who wrote the Bible, but some things we can say with certainty. The people who wrote the Bible had powerful encounters with God. Their lives were changed by their faith, and they wanted to pass their faith on to future generations.

BIBLICAL TOOLS
- Read: Acts 7:54–8:3, Acts 9:1-20, and 2 Corinthians 11:22-27.
- Look up Paul/Saul and Timothy in a Bible dictionary.
- Make notes about what you learned about Paul and Timothy.

How does the information you learned about Paul affect how you read these passages?

What difference does it make if you know about the people who wrote the Bible?

CLOSING PRAYER

Loving God, be our guide. With each question we ask and with every Scripture we read, may we rely on your Spirit as we more deeply explore your Holy Bible. Amen.

NOTES

2. What? Genre

Why Does This Matter?

In the 1999 movie *Galaxy Quest*, the washed-up stars of a popular 1970s science fiction show are visited by aliens. The aliens beam the actors into their spaceship and explain that they've discovered their "historical documents" and have proudly modeled their society after them. What they've really discovered are reruns of the science fiction show. They've made a mistake in genre.

It's an easy mistake to make. The television show is a broadcast from another society, in another time and place. But as this lighthearted comedy illustrates, making a mistake in genre can skew one's entire interpretation. Modern readers of the Bible face a similar challenge. We have stories and writings that have come to us from another society, in another time and place. One of the first major questions we face when trying to interpret these texts is that of genre.

Some examples of biblical genres include: poetry, worship songs, historical records, parables, narratives, satire, letters, and apocalyptic literature. Each genre has its own forms and style by which it is identified. Biblical poetry often uses parallelism, hyperbole, and metaphors. Letters often identify the author and audience in the first lines. Historical records list kings and events.

Some genres are easier to identify than others. Satire, for example, is often tricky. Think of how many people post articles on social media from satirical news websites without realizing they aren't true—and those are articles from our own time and place! Bible readers have even more difficulty identifying certain genres because of our lack of familiarity with the social and literary conventions of biblical societies.

Because of those barriers, we often must rely on biblical scholars who have researched other ancient writings to help us identify genre. However, you don't have to become experts in the forms of biblical case law to understand the Ten Commandments. The important thing is to simply recognize that genre matters and know how to investigate biblical genres.

What Is the Bible, Anyway?

What kind of book is the Bible? Or, more accurately, what kinds of books are in the Bible? In which sections of a bookstore or a library do you think you would find each book of the Bible, if they were separated?

These questions are all about genre, or the category to which a piece of writing belongs. We can tell a book's genre

14

Parable—Story made up to teach

by reading it carefully and looking for clues. Just as today we know a story that starts out "Once upon a time ..." is likely to be a fairy tale, in biblical times, authors had their own ways of signaling which genre they were using.

Why does it matter what genre a book is? Well, knowing the genre of a book can completely change our interpretation of it. For example, if we thought a fairy tale was a news report, we might become frightened, missing the point of the story. Or, if we thought a list of telephone numbers was a secret code, we might spend hours trying to figure it out. Genre is important because it tells you how to understand and respond to a piece of writing.

Translating Genre

Did you know that the original Hebrew text of the Old Testament didn't have vowels, capitalization, punctuation, verse numbers, or formatting?

Vowels and paragraph divisions were added to the Hebrew text between the sixth and tenth centuries—hundreds of years after the original texts were written. The chapter and verse numbers we use today were added in the twelfth century. All the rest of the punctuation—indents, question marks, quotation marks, and everything else—is up to modern translators to decide. These details are important because vocabulary, punctuation, and formatting are major clues to genre.

Check out Jonah, Chapter 2, in two different translations of the Bible—the Common English Bible and the King James Version.

What differences do you notice between each version? How did each translator communicate the genre of the passage, as he or she saw it? Which interpretation do you agree with?

Why don't you give it a try yourself? Without looking it up, take the following text from Jonah 1:7b-10. Add your own punctuation, formatting, and verse numbers. Then compare it to what's printed in your Bible.

THEY CAST LOTS AND THE LOT FELL ON JONAH. SO THEY SAID TO HIM, "TELL US SINCE YOU'RE THE CAUSE OF THIS EVIL HAPPENING TO US, WHAT DO YOU DO AND WHERE ARE YOU FROM? WHAT'S YOUR COUNTRY AND OF WHAT PEOPLE ARE YOU? HE SAID TO THEM I'M A HEBREW, I WORSHIP THE LORD, THE GOD OF HEAVEN WHO MADE THE SEA AND THE DRY LAND, THEN THE MEN WERE TERRIFIED AND SAID TO HIM, WHAT HAVE YOU DONE? THE MEN KNEW THAT JONAH WAS FLEEING FROM THE LORD BECAUSE HE HAD TOLD THEM.

BIBLICAL TOOLS

Study Bibles and Bible commentaries are written by scholars who study the Bible in its historical context. But remember that commentators are just people, sharing their best interpretations with us. You bring your own insights and questions to the Bible. It's okay to disagree with a commentary.

- Look up the Book of Jonah in a study Bible and Bible commentary. Typically, possible genres are discussed in the introduction to a book.
- Look up Jonah in a Bible dictionary.

What genres do the commentators assign to Jonah? How would your interpretation of the story be different depending on the genre you assume?

Why does genre matter when you're interpreting the Bible? What difference does it make?

Figuring out the genre of a part of the Bible is important, but it's often a guessing game. How do you feel about the possibility of mistaking the genre of a book?

How important is it for you to know what the original author meant? Do you think the Bible can change genres and meanings over time? Why or why not?

Closing Prayer

God of us all, we give thanks for the courage of those gathered here. Inspire our hearts to find you in your Holy Word. May our time together help us live as faithful people in your name. Amen.

NOTES

3. When? Context

Why Does This Matter?

When children are in grade school, their reading skills improve and they begin to encounter new vocabulary. They're taught to work out the meaning of unfamiliar words by using "context clues." Many adults still do this reflexively, because they know that words can take on different meanings, depending on the context. Gross can mean "yucky" when your child says it, but it typically means "the overall total" when it's printed on your paycheck.

The meaning of any given word is dependent on the words around it, because languages are systems. And languages are produced by societies, which are systems of people. The meanings of words, phrases, and whole stories change as society changes. Take the word *nice*. In the fourteenth century, nice meant "ignorant" or "foolish." Over hundreds of years, the word has changed meanings several times, landing on "agreeable." An insult has become a compliment.

When modern readers encounter a biblical text, contexts collide. It's easy to forget that the Bible was created in another language and society when today we're reading the Bible on our cell phones. Most modern readers bring our own linguistic and cultural understandings to bear on the Bible without even realizing that we are doing so. We only tend to remember the contextual divide between ourselves and the text when the stories are strange or archaic. When this happens, we can't seamlessly absorb them into our modern worldview.

The truth is, context always matters in interpretation, whether or not the reader is aware of it. Anytime someone picks up the Bible, there are at least three contexts to consider—the literary context, the historical context, and the cultural context. We are already familiar with our own cultural context. How do we become familiar with the literary and historical contexts of the Bible?

Historians, biblical archaeologists, linguists, and other scholars have done the research. Bible dictionaries, commentaries, and handbooks contain condensed versions of that research. Using these tools, we can discover the context clues that shed new light on biblical texts.

Contextualize It

context (noun) \kän-tekst\ | the group of conditions that exist where and when something happens. From the Latin contextere, *"to weave together."*

What's up? What's down? What's going on around you? Are you a person walking on the sidewalk? Are you a bird flying in the air? Are you an alien living on another planet? Whatever is happening in your world, whatever circumstances affect your everyday life, that's your historical context.

In most American cities, our context includes things like:

- the fact that we can take a car, bus, bike, or walk to work;
- the ability to instantly get in touch with people hundreds of miles away through email, phones, and social media;
- the fact that most of us in our community learn how to read; and
- the ability to buy fresh fruits and vegetables from the grocery store year-round.

These realities are so common that many people don't realize that they haven't always been true, and still aren't true in every culture. For most people, their context feels like the way things should be. They don't even realize there's another way of doing things until they meet someone from another culture or experience the other culture themselves.

When we read the Bible, we're like time travelers entering another culture. We're reading stories, prophecies, and letters from completely different contexts, passed down to us through hundreds of years. Nobody reading the Bible today remembers what it was like to live in Jerusalem when King David ruled, or in Persia when Esther was queen, or in Nazareth when Jesus was growing up.

So, when we read the Bible today, we have to work to contextualize it. We have to put the story back into its own context. First, we learn about the time and place, when and where the story was written, so we can understand what it might have meant at the time. We also put the story in its literary context by reading what comes before and after the story. Then, we can think about what it might mean today, in our own context.

Alien Archaeologist

Imagine you are an alien from a distant planet. You've landed on planet Earth. You begin exploring and encounter the following objects/items. From your alien context, write what you think each item might be for. Remember, as an alien, you know absolutely NOTHING about human culture.

Hair Dryer—

Carousel—

Vacuum Cleaner—

Fishing Pole—

Clothes Hanger—

Before and After

Whenever you study a Bible passage, it's important to do a before-and-after check. That means reading a few verses before the section and a few verses after the section to see if there's any important information that can help you understand the passage.

Another option is to look up the introduction to the book you're reading in a study Bible or commentary. Most of the time, Bible scholars make an outline of the book. They break it into sections based on major themes. This can be done by checking to see what section your passage is in. What's it called? How does it fit into the book as a whole?

Biblical Tools

- Look up Luke 6:1-11. What do you think are the main points of this passage?
- Read the section before (Luke 5:33-39).
- Read the section after (Luke 6:12-19).
- Explore any questions you have, using study Bibles, commentaries, and Bible dictionaries.

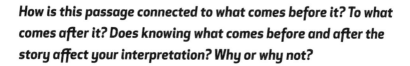

How is this passage connected to what comes before it? To what comes after it? Does knowing what comes before and after the story affect your interpretation? Why or why not?

Why does the historical context of the Bible matter? What difference does it make?

Do you think the Bible can still be meaningful to your daily life when you live in such a different historical context? Why or why not?

Closing Prayer

Holy God, as we wander through your word help us to seek and find you. You are the meaning maker of our lives, and it is through your word we discover new ways of living as your faithful people. Amen.

NOTES

4. Where? Geography

Why Does This Matter

When it snows in Texas, everything closes. When it snows in Massachusetts, it's business as usual. When urbanites in New York talk about the weather, they're making small talk. When farmers in Kansas talk about the weather, they're talking about work. When it's windy in North Carolina, it makes for a nice breeze. When it's windy in Oklahoma, it could be dangerous. Everyone's life is shaped, to varying degrees, by their geography.

Modern city dwelling folks are less likely to be aware of the effects of geography, but people in Bible times were sharply aware of their relationship with the land. For them, geography was a life-and-death subject, not a subject in school. People in Bible times didn't have maps as we know them, scaled guides of the local landscape. Without a bird's-eye view, the biblical authors' only way of knowing their geography was to explore it and occasionally get lost in it.

Long trips were inherently dangerous, because the prospect of becoming lost without access to food or water was real. Food preservation was difficult, so travelers relied almost entirely on the hospitality of strangers to feed and shelter them. For long trips or moves, people traveled in large family groups and brought their livestock with them. Travel was arduous. In short, being away from or without your own plot of arable land made you vulnerable.

Even when the Israelites did settle in Canaan, their survival was not guaranteed. Long droughts like the one in 1 Kings 17-18 threatened the Israelites' survival. No wonder the Israelites placed such spiritual and religious value on the land as God's promised blessing. The land was life. Today, this poignancy is gone from many modern people's relationship with the land. As a result, we often overlook geography. Imagining the biblical landscape enriches our ability to enter into the biblical narrative. Stories become more textured when we imagine the sensory experience of wandering in the desert or sailing on the Mediterranean. We better understand the urgency of Mary and Joseph's flight to Egypt, or the passion that the magi must have felt to travel all that way. In short, biblical geography reveals a new layer of meaning.

Bible Geography

When you hear the word geography, what do you think? If you're like most people, you think of maps. But geography is about much more than national borders or navigation.

The geography, or landscape, of your homeland shapes your life in important ways. Your local geography determines the food you eat, the clothes you wear, the type of house you live in, and more.

Now that we live in a globally connected world, we're not completely limited by our geography. We can eat a banana grown in Jamaica, pull on a T-shirt made in Cambodia, and ride in a car made in Japan—all before we go to work. Even so, it's likely that if you live on the Maine coast, seafood is a regular part of your diet; and if you live in Alaska, you own a heavy coat; and if you live in Kansas, you know where to take shelter during a tornado.

How much our geography affects us differs, depending on where we live. But in biblical times, geography played a much bigger role in people's lives. Their lives were determined by their local geography. They ate whatever food they could grow or raise on the land. They wore whatever clothing they could make from local plants or animal skins. They built houses out of bricks made from local mud or stone.

Most of the stories in the Bible take place in Israel, a small land, but packed with diversity. The land of ancient Israel contained high mountains (Mount Hermon is 9,000 feet!) as well as the Dead Sea, the lowest point on the earth's surface. Parts of Israel were dry and desert-like, and other parts were humid and close to the Mediterranean Sea.

Wheat, barley, figs, pistachios, grapes, and olive trees were abundant. The Israelites snacked on bread, olive oil, fruit, and nuts.

Sheep and goats were able to survive on the dry, broken terrain, so Israelite clothes were often made from wool or leather.

BIBLICAL TOOLS
- Find Exodus 16:1-21 in the Bible.
- Look up maps using a study Bible and Bible atlas.

How do you think geography might affect the experience the Israelites had wandering in the wilderness? What would you like to find out about the geography of their journey?

What information have you gathered? How does this information shed light on our story?

How familiar were you with the biblical landscape before now? What's one thing you learned that you didn't know before?

What does the wilderness symbolize to you? Have you ever been in a spiritual wilderness?

How does learning more about the literal wilderness help you understand the symbolic wilderness? What does this story teach us about being in a wilderness and relying on God?

Closing Prayer

God of promise, whose grace and guidance brought your people from out of the wilderness into a land of promise, we journey alongside you to discover your word for our lives. May we always seek to follow you. Amen.

NOTES

---

5. Why? Interpretation

Why Does This Matter?

Interpretation is the work of the human brain. Our brains are constantly at work interpreting the world around us and all forms of communication therein. Imagine two people hiking in the woods. They each see a large, brown form ahead. The first person interprets the shape as a fallen tree trunk, and hardly reacts. The second person interprets the shape as a bear, and quickly becomes frightened. Each person's interpretation of the shape happened in fractions of a second, unconsciously.

When we read the Bible, our brains process the text through their already existing frameworks. These might be called our "interpretive lenses" because they filter information before it even arrives at our conscious brains. This is similar to eyeglass lenses filtering visual images before our brain processes them. It's our job to identify our interpretive lenses and be aware of them as we read the text.

Only then will we be able to understand how we can read the same text as another person and then sometimes arrive at opposing interpretations.

In addition to interpretive lenses, there are interpretive layers we must acknowledge. The biblical text arrives in our hands at the end of a centuries-long process of interpretation. Remember, between us and the original audiences of the Bible, there are translators, canonizers, scribes and copyists, editors, authors, and oral storytellers. Each of these represents a separate interpretive layer; each person who wrote, edited, copied, canonized, and translated the text made interpretive decisions.

Through all these layers and lenses, we read the Bible and make meaning from it. The task is, at times, daunting. This is why belief in the guidance of the Holy Spirit in hearing and understanding God's word is so essential. It's also why reading the Bible in community is crucial to faithful interpretation. We read our holy Scriptures in community so that we might hear the interpretation of people in different life situations. Only then can all the facets of God's word come to life. You and your faith community have an important part in the sacredness of interpreting the Bible.

We have lots of tools to help us investigate the meaning of biblical passages. In the end, it's up to us to determine, through prayer and reflection, what the Bible means to our lives today.

LAYERS AND LENSES

There are layers to interpretation. There are also lenses. Lenses and layers. Layers and lenses. This can get confusing at times. Here's a breakdown of the lenses and layers of Bible interpretation:

Layers

Between the original author and the modern reader, the Bible passed through many hands. By the time the Bible gets to you, it's already gone through several layers of interpretation, which have influenced the meaning.

The Translators—The Bible was originally written in Hebrew, Greek, and occasionally other languages. You can read the Bible in English thanks to the work of translators. If you've ever learned a foreign language, you know that translation can be tricky. Words and phrases in one language don't translate neatly into another. Take the English phrase "I ran into him at the store." If you translated that word-by-word into another language, the reader might imagine someone literally sprinting into another person. In order to get the true meaning across, the translator needs to figure out how to convey the idea of coincidentally meeting someone at the store. Translators have to decide the best way to communicate all kinds of words and phrases in another language, and that's interpretation.

The Canonizers—How did the Bible become the Bible? Why were some stories, letters, and gospels preserved while others faded into obscurity? The answer lies with the canonizers. The canonizers are the people who decided which books were important enough to be in the canon or the Christian Bible, and what order they should go in. Most of the canonizers were Christian leaders during the second to fourth centuries.

The Scribes—Back before the printing press was invented, each copy of the Bible was written by hand by a scribe. Scribes carefully wrote every word exactly as they saw it in their original manuscript. But the scribes were human. Sometimes they made mistakes. Sometimes they intentionally altered the text to make up for what they thought was an error. As archaeologists unearth and historians preserve ancient scrolls, they can compare them to discover the variations.

The Editors—Many of the books of the Bible draw from different sources. The editors of the Bible took many stories—written and passed down orally—and wove them into one story. Biblical scholars can sometimes tell when an editor has combined two stories, because the writing style changes abruptly.

Lenses

In addition to layers, there are also lenses of interpretation. Everybody wears metaphorical glasses when they read. The "lenses" you read through influence how you interpret the story. Your lenses are shaped by life experiences.

A person who is afraid of storms might read Jesus calming the storm with a different lens then someone who loves the rain. Someone with an anxiety disorder will read Jesus' encouragement not to worry differently than others. Everyone has a different set of lenses. That's why everyone reads the Bible differently.

BIBLICAL TOOLS

Did you know that one of the most debated parts of the Bible is in the very first chapter? Genesis 1 is a poem about Creation. The poet says that God created humanity in "God's own image." For centuries, Jews and Christians have tried to understand what that means. What's your interpretation?

- Read Verse 27, and what comes after it, in Genesis 1:27-31.
- Read it from a few different translations so you have a sense of what the original language could have meant.
- Use a different tool to investigate the passage, choosing between a study Bible, a commentary, a Bible dictionary, and a concordance.

How does this information shed light on our story?

Now that you've investigated other people's interpretations of the meaning of "God's image," what do you think it means to be created in God's image? How does this passage affect how you interact with others, especially those who interpret the Bible differently than you?

What do lenses and layers have to do with biblical interpretation? What difference do they make?

Closing Prayer

God of the Bible, you have created us as unique children of God. Each of us is held by your holy hands. May we remember to see you in all living things. Your word is a living document which reminds us of your vision for the world. We are thankful. Amen.

NOTES

6. How? Read Closely

Why Does This Matter?

When we read the Bible today, we have turnable pages or scrollable screens. We can have Bible verses delivered to our email in-boxes. We can study the Bible with apps that show us multiple translations at once. Our Bible ease-of-use rating is off the charts. It's hard sometimes to imagine the effort that went into creating these ancient texts. It's even hard for us, who have always lived in a world with printing presses, to imagine the arduous task of copying manuscripts by hand.

In our biblical ancestors' economy of words, each word held much more value than it does now. The people who wrote, edited, and copied the biblical text didn't take a single word for granted. Every word was carefully chosen by authors, copied by scribes, and memorized by illiterate people of faith. When we practice reading the Bible closely, we honor the careful work of our ancestors.

We also strengthen our faith by paying attention. Simone Weil, a French Catholic theologian, argued that prayer is the highest form of paying attention, of opening oneself to God. Any lesser form of paying attention, such as studying the Bible, only strengthens one's ability to pay attention in prayer.

Many of us read the Bible and begin drawing conclusions about the meaning before we even finish reading. This tendency to interpret on autopilot impedes the process of paying close attention to a text. Why would we need to read it carefully if we already know what it means?

Christians who read the Bible carefully are often surprised by what they find. For example, in nearly every nativity set there are three magi figures. If most Christians were asked why, they'd respond that the Bible says three magi visited Jesus. But the Bible doesn't say there were three magi. Much of what we assume the Bible says comes from our cultural Christian traditions. This is a small example. In other instances, a failure to read carefully might yield a more drastic difference in interpretation. The goal is to slow down and read carefully by paying attention to the four possible meanings, or "senses," that Jewish and Christian interpreters have historically looked for in the biblical text.

Four Meanings, One Text

How many different ways can you read one passage of the Bible? Well, since the Middle Ages, some Jewish and Christian Bible interpreters have believed there are at least four ways. Their lists didn't match up perfectly, but each tradition listed four unique ways to interpret Scripture. Here's a mash-up of the two lists:

The literal, or plain meaning—Christian interpreters called this the literal sense. Rabbis called this the *peshat*, from the Hebrew word for "surface." This way of reading takes the text at face value.

The comparative meaning—The comparative meaning is what the meaning passages take on when read in connection with other parts of the Bible. Christian interpreters called this the allegorical or typological sense. Rabbis called this the *derash*, from the Hebrew word for "inquire, seek." This way of reading looks at a passage as a part of the whole Bible, not just by itself.

The deeper symbolic meaning—Christian interpreters called this the moral sense, or the "moral of the story." Rabbis called this the *remez*, from the Hebrew word for "hints." This way of reading looks for meaningful symbols and lessons that can be drawn from the passage.

The secret, mystical meaning—Christian interpreters called this the anagogical sense. They believed some passages contained hidden prophecies about heaven, hell, and the second coming of Christ. Rabbis called this the *sod*, from the Hebrew word for "secret." They believed this meaning of the text could only be revealed to a reader through divine inspiration.

INTERPRET A FAIRY TALE

Let's try out the first three forms of interpretation with a common story—"Little Red Riding Hood." If it's been a while since you've heard the story, here's a recap:

Little Red Riding Hood is a little girl named after the fancy, red cloak she wears. One day, her mother sends her to visit her granny with a basket of food. Her mother warns her to stay on the path through the forest.

A Big Bad Wolf is also in the forest. He spies Red and follows her for a while. He approaches her and asks her where she's going. Red tells the Wolf she's visiting her granny. The Wolf suggests that she pick some flowers for Granny. While Red is picking flowers, the Wolf goes ahead of her and eats her granny!

The Wolf puts on Granny's clothes and waits for Red to arrive. Red notices immediately how different Granny looks. She comments, "My, what big eyes you have!" The Wolf responds, "The better to see you with, my dear." Red says, "My, what big ears you have!" The Wolf responds, "The better to hear you with, my dear." Red exclaims, "My, what big teeth you have!" The Wolf growls, "The better to eat you with!"

Then he proceeds to eat Red as well. Fortunately, a hunter drops by, cuts open the Big Bad Wolf, and rescues Little Red Riding Hood and her granny.

Try it out:

- Literal meaning—tell the story in your own words.
- Comparative meaning—are there any connections between this story and other fairy tales? Do Big Bad Wolves appear in other stories? What about young girls? Grandmothers? Forests? Think of all the connections you can.
- Symbolic meaning—What's the "moral of the story?" What are the symbols in the story? What do they represent?

When you're interpreting the literal sense of a biblical passage, you can feel like you are stating the obvious. That's okay! It's an important part of Bible study. Because the truth is, most of the time the literal meaning of the text is obvious. But sometimes it isn't. It's always good to check for a basic level of understanding by restating the main points of the passage in your own words.

BIBLICAL TOOLS

- Read Genesis 22:1-19. Then answer the questions:
  1. Who is in the story?
  2. Where does the story take place?
  3. What are the main points of the plot?
  4. How does the story end?

- Look up the related passages listed in a study Bible (these are usually found in the margin). You might also look up interesting words found in the story in the concordance to see how they are used elsewhere.
- Consider the symbolic meaning of the story by reading the notes in a study Bible.

Do you think it's possible for the four ways of reading the Bible to contradict one another? Why do you think Jewish and Christian interpreters came up with these four ways of looking at a story?

Why should we read the Bible carefully? Why do we need to pay attention to the different kinds of meanings in the Bible?

Now that you've explored the first three senses of the story, it's time to explore the "secret sense." What does this story in Genesis 22:1-19 mean to you? What is God saying to you through this story? Does it hold special meaning for you? Why or why not?

Closing Prayer

Mighty God, you are bigger than anything we can imagine. Yet, your wisdom and your teachings give us a glimpse into who you are and how we can deeply connect to you and to one another. Amen.

NOTES

7. How? Reread

Why Does This Matter?

The first six lessons of this study teach us how to analyze the Bible by drawing on the findings of historical criticism, literary analysis, biblical archaeology, and more. Those methods of study are invaluable to the modern reader. Those methods also illuminate the biblical text by clarifying its origins, decentering our modern point of view, and drawing us into the strange and exciting world of the original authors and audiences. By studying our ancestors' encounters with God, we open ourselves to our own encounters with God.

Now it's time to turn our focus away from the world of the authors and toward our own responses as readers. Reader-response criticism is a method of interpretation that centers the readers' experience of a text and role in meaning making. Reader-response criticism balances a tendency to focus entirely on the original authors of the Bible, alongside the vital role of the reader.

If the biblical text is the "living word of God," then its meaning cannot stagnate in ancient Israel. It must also be capable of making new meaning as people of faith experience the text. Both the historical context and the reader's context are important in biblical interpretation. This belief is not a newfangled theological response to changing times. It is an ancient belief that is fundamental to Christian biblical interpretation. As early as the New Testament, Christians reinterpreted the Hebrew Scriptures in light of their experience of the resurrected Christ.

By the third century, a Christian theologian named Origen taught a method of prayerfully reading the Scriptures through the lens of Christ, as a way to draw closer to God. He called this method *lectio divina* or "divine reading," and throughout the centuries, Christian monks have distilled the general method into four steps: *lectio* (read), *meditatio* (meditate), *oratio* (pray), and *contemplatio* (contemplate). This basic method has been adapted into various steps for different audiences. It typically involves reading the same Scripture several times in a meditative fashion.

Today we're focusing on what we bring to biblical interpretation. Each of us brings our unique perspective to every passage we interpret. God speaks to each of us through the Bible, so our life experiences are an important part of interpretation.

Divine Reading

Over the past few weeks, we've learned a lot about how the Bible was created. You've become a modern-day biblical scholar! Now it's time to shift the focus. Let's talk about you.

The Bible isn't just about the people who created it. If it were, why would we still be reading it after all these years? The Bible is also about you. It's your sacred story, and it's your life and faith that is affected by how you relate to the Bible.

When you pick up the Bible, you're not just reading about your spiritual ancestors' encounters with God. You're also opening yourself to having your own encounter with God. The Holy Spirit speaks to us in many ways, and one of those ways is through Scripture.

Today we're going to investigate where you are in the biblical story. What is God saying to you through the Bible? How can you grow closer to God and Jesus Christ through reading Scripture?

Read—Read the passage carefully. Notice any words or phrases that stick out in your mind.

Meditate—In this step, let your brain get creative with the passage. As you or someone else reads the passage again, be creative with art supplies, rewrite a verse, or think deeply as you go over the passage in your mind.

Pray—In this step, have a conversation with God. You can read the passage as though you're praying it, or you can simply ask, "God, what are you saying to me through this passage today?"

Contemplate—In this step, listen for God's response to your prayer and meditation. As the passage is read a final time, quiet your mind and be open to any response you sense.

We have lots of tools to help us develop deeper meaning of biblical passages. In the end, it's up to us to determine, through prayer and reflection, what the Bible means to our lives today.

BIBLICAL TOOLS

- Practice *Lectio Divina*. Choose some artistic materials you would like to use during meditation, prayer, and contemplation of the passage.
- Find Psalm 139:1-6 in your Bible.
- Light a candle before you begin. Turn on quiet instrumental music if you choose.
- Read the passage out loud. Allow a few minutes of silence and use your art supplies to meditate on the passage.
- Read the passage again. Allow a few minutes of silence. Pray about whatever the passage brings up for you.
- Acquire a set of meditation beads. (You can easily make meditation beads by stringing yarn with eight to ten pony beads and knotting each end.)
- During this last reading, we will listen for God to speak to us through the passage. Listening in silence can be a difficult task for busy minds. Meditation beads give our hands something to do as we listen quietly.

What part of the passage "shimmered" or stuck out to you?

What was the easiest part of that reading for you? What was difficult for you? What insights did you gain from this way of reading Scripture?

What did you hear from God as you practiced divine reading today? How will you respond to what you heard?

What does divine reading have to do with biblical interpretation? Where are you in the biblical story?

Closing Prayer

God, when we pay close attention to your words, we can find our place in the Holy Scriptures. May we remember that this is our story, and if we just listen we can hear your voice calling us to share your story with others. Amen.

NOTES

8. How? Read Together

Why Does This Matter?

We think of the Bible as one book, because we have the luxury of reading it in bound copies. Even those who study the Bible, and recognize it as a collection of disparate texts created over centuries, tend to speak of the "biblical narrative," or "overarching story of the text." Those may be helpful shorthand ways to refer to our inherited faith, but they don't do justice to the diversity of voices within the biblical canon.

Cohesive narratives are created by one author, or by authors working in concert. The biblical authors didn't have the luxury of checking in with one another to discuss where the enterprise was headed. Some biblical authors clearly had access to other texts that would eventually become part of the Bible. But the collection of texts that make up the canon are piecemeal perspectives on the story of Israel and the Jesus movement that emerged from it.

If those who canonized the Scriptures had truly preferred a single, cohesive narrative, they could have omitted books, edited others, and crafted a much smoother story. Instead, they carefully preserved a library of diverse, and at times contradictory, perspectives. Rather than giving us an epic saga, they gave us an opportunity for epic conversation.

We who have inherited bound copies of the "book" known as the Holy Bible have been given an immeasurable gift. We have a bird's-eye view of the sacred stories of our spiritual ancestors. We can see the connections, the comparisons, and the inter-canonical conversations that those who created the text never could have seen. We can weave multiple threads into one larger conversation. But it's important to remember the integrity of each thread on its own. In our eagerness to unearth the "one story" of the Bible, we may find ourselves cutting away threads that seem unnecessary or stubbornly unwilling to be woven into our narrative. We can make the mistake of Martin Luther, who was so convinced that the story of the Bible was "justification by faith alone," he concluded that the Book of James had to go. Rather than glossing over the Bible's dissonant voices, our ancestors invite us to wrestle with them, enter the conversation, and find our own place in the story of faith.

Canon Connections

Back in the days of the early church, being called a "Marcionite" was a big insult. Marcionites followed a man named Marcion, who argued that the teachings of Jesus were completely incompatible with the God of the Old Testament.

Thus, he believed that the God of the Old Testament could not be Jesus' father.

Marcion's teachings were rejected by the early church. Even though church leaders recognized some differences between the Hebrew Scriptures and the Gospels, they also saw deep connections. They believed that the teachings of Jesus built upon the teachings in the Hebrew Scriptures. Rather than throwing out the Old Testament, early church leaders reinterpreted it in light of Jesus' Jewish heritage and teachings.

It can be tempting to view the Bible as one epic story, with a plot that perfectly progresses with each book. Marcion thought that's what the Bible should be, so he threw out the parts that didn't match his idea of the biblical story. As we've learned, the Bible is not one big and long story. Instead, the Bible is more like an invitation for an in-depth conversation. There are diverse perspectives, and they don't always easily fit together. But the many voices of the Bible help us understand the many angles of truth.

The parts of the Bible that don't seem to fit are often just another way of looking at the same truth. For many Jews, it didn't seem possible to say that a person was God, or even the Son of God. That concept just didn't fit into their understanding of God. But Christians said that it was possible. They reinterpreted the Hebrew Scriptures in light of Jesus and found new meanings. Can you see both perspectives?

Today, Christians read the New Testament alongside the Old Testament all the time. Some churches follow a lectionary. The lectionary always has readings from the Old and New Testaments, because Christians believe the Old and New Testaments talk to each other. Scripture is a conversation, which allows us to explore different parts of that conversation through the lectionary.

Psalm 23 is what you might call a classic. Chances are, you've heard it before. You may even have memorized it when you were younger. Take a moment to refresh your memory:

THE LORD IS MY SHEPHERD

[1]The LORD is my shepherd.
      I lack nothing.
[2]He lets me rest in grassy meadows;
      he leads me to restful waters;
      [3]he keeps me alive.
  He guides me in proper paths
      for the sake of his good name.
[4]Even when I walk
      through the darkest valley,
      I fear no danger because you are with me.
Your rod and your staff—
      they protect me.
[5]You set a table for me
      right in front of my enemies.
You bathe my head in oil;
      my cup is so full it spills over!
[6]Yes, goodness and faithful love
      will pursue me all the days of my life,
      and I will live in the LORD's house
      as long as I live.

Did you know that one of the prophets sampled from Psalm 23? Ezekiel 34:1-16 uses this image of God as Israel's shepherd to speak out against unjust leaders. Check out verses 11-16.

[11]The LORD God proclaims: I myself will search for my flock and seek them out. [12]As a shepherd seeks out the flock when some in the flock have been scattered, so will I seek out my flock. I will rescue them from all the places where they were scattered during the time of clouds and thick darkness. [13]I will gather and lead them out from the countries and peoples, and I will bring them to their own fertile land. I will feed them on Israel's highlands, along the riverbeds, and in all the inhabited places. [14]I will feed them in good pasture, and their sheepfold will be there, on Israel's lofty highlands. On Israel's highlands, they will lie down in a secure fold and feed on green pastures. [15]I myself will feed my flock and make them lie down. This is what the LORD God says. [16]I will seek out the lost, bring back the strays, bind up the wounded, and strengthen the weak. But the fat and the strong I will destroy, because I will tend my sheep with justice.

> **BIBLICAL TOOLS**
> - Find John 10:1-16 in your Bibles.
> - Try to better understand the different characters: the Good Shepherd, the ordinary shepherds, the thieves, the sheep. Gather information using the study Bibles, commentary, Bible dictionary, and concordance.

What connections do you see between Ezekiel 34:11-16 and Psalm 23? What do those connections teach you about God?

How does our knowledge of the Ezekiel passage and the Psalm help us understand what Jesus is saying in John 10:1-16?

Why are the connections between biblical passages important? What difference do they make?

Does thinking of the Bible as a conversation rather than a story change how you interact with it? Do you see yourself as a part of the biblical conversation? Why or why not?

Closing Prayer

God who is still speaking, may we remember to be in continuous conversation with you. Help us to find ourselves in the ongoing biblical conversation so that we may find truth, knowledge, and wisdom on our journey with you. Amen.

NOTES